— Praise for Jacks(

"Jackson Dean Chase has found a place on my shelf, the **dark** corner, where I hide my **twisted little secrets**."
—*Tome Tender*

"He **continues to amaze me** with his creativity and darkness."
—*Fang Freakin' Tastic Reviews*

— Praise for Bukowski's Ghost —

"With *Bukowski's Ghost,* Jackson Dean Chase invokes the spirit of the greatest poet of our time with the respect and admiration he deserves. This is an honest, intense, and remarkable collection by **a fresh and powerful new voice**."
—*Terry Trueman, Printz Honor author of* Stuck in Neutral

"Poems immersed in **the despair of the lost, broken, and lonely**."
—*Kindle reviewer (UK)*

"...**Haunting** enough **I can feel Charles Bukowski's breath** on the back of my neck."
—*Kindle reviewer*

— Praise for Love at the Bottom of the Litter Box —

"If you love cats, if you've ever struggled to make it, then **you will love this book**."
—*Kindle reviewer*

"Jackson Dean Chase really **lets you see and feel his true self** in this book."
—*Kindle reviewer*

— Praise for Christmas Eve in the Drunk Tank —

"A crazy collection of weird winter and holiday-themed poems **sure to bring a twisted smile to the face of Charles Bukowski fans**."
—*Kindle reviewer*

— Books by Jackson Dean Chase —

Poetry

Raw Underground Poetry series:
   #1 Bukowski's Ghost
   #2 Love at the Bottom of the Litter Box
   #3 Christmas Eve in the Drunk Tank
   #4 Be the Magic

Fiction

Beyond the Dome series:
   #0 Hard Times in Dronetown
   #1 Drone
   #2 Warrior (coming soon)

Young Adult Best Sellers series:
   #1 Young Adult Fiction Best Sellers

Young Adult Horror series:
   #1 Come to the Cemetery
   #2 The Werewolf Wants Me
   #3 The Haunting of Hex House
   #4 Gore Girls: Twisted Tales & Poems
   #5 Lost Girls: Twisted Tales & Poems
   #6 Horror Girls: Twisted Tales & Poems
   #7 Killer Young Adult Fiction (complete series + extras)

Non-Fiction

How to Write Realistic Fiction series:
   #1 How to Write Realistic Characters
   #2 How to Write Realistic Men

Writers' Phrase Book series:
   #1 Horror Writers' Phrase Book
   #2 Post-Apocalypse Writers' Phrase Book
   #3 Action Writers' Phrase Book

— RAW UNDERGROUND POETRY —

BE THE
MAGIC

(Poems to Ignite and Inspire)

JACKSON DEAN
CHASE

www.JacksonDeanChase.com

For my magic, and yours

A book like this owes its existence to many I have met along the way, in this world and the next: friends and family, ghosts and spirits, and yes, even enemies—real and imagined. The struggle has made me stronger. Thank you.

- Thanks to Charles Bukowski, for teaching me to love poetry.
- Thanks to my editor, C. Graves, for shaping my talent.
- Special thanks to my incredible Launch Team: Jen Crews, Melanie Marsh, Sherry Rentschler, Tina Simon, and Julie Stafford.

First Printing, December 2015

ISBN-13: 978-1522925101

ISBN-10: 1522925104

Published by Jackson Dean Chase, Inc.

Printed by CreateSpace

PUBLISHER'S NOTE

"Bold Visions of Dark Places" is a trademark of Jackson Dean Chase, Inc.

This is a work of fiction. Names, characters, places, and incidents are products of the author's imagination or are used fictitiously. Any resemblance to actual events or locales or persons, living or dead, is entirely coincidental.

Want FREE BOOKS? Visit the Author at:
www.JacksonDeanChase.com

— CONTENTS —

— INTRODUCTION —

"Passion fuels destiny."

The most important thing in life is to find your passion, harness it, and realize your dreams. All else springs from that one act: happiness, love, respect, career. It doesn't matter what your passion is, so long as it brings joy to you and at least one other person. I say this because although it may begin with you creating for yourself, it cannot end there, or your passion is a selfish thing, a flower behind a locked door.

I am not suggesting you share your work before it is ready—quite the opposite. Take the time you need to develop your passion, knowing it will never be "perfect," but it will be good enough and worth sharing.

Your passion is your magic, your gift to the world. Some will reject you for daring to be authentic and fearless. Forget them. There are many more who will be drawn to you and accept you for who you are. Embrace them and the power they give you.

Your Fellow Magician,
Jackson Dean Chase
www.JacksonDeanChase.com

WAKE UP!

Wake up!

You're more than you are now,
more than your current job demands,
what your friends and family expect.
You're a living, breathing supernova
of untapped potential.

   Wake up and realize it.

FOR THOSE WHO ARE DIFFERENT

Everyone who thinks different,
   looks different,
   acts different,
must find some way to fit in
   for their safety,
and some way to stand out
   for their sanity.

People Aren't Perfect

You will be mocked for being you who are,
for looking like you do.
For not being the kind of "perfect" you see
 in magazines, in movies,
 or on TV.
But the truth is these "perfect" people are anything but.
They are just like us, only they have money for:
 plastic surgery,
 personal trainers,
 photoshop experts,
 makeup artists,
 and fancy clothes.
But that's all they have.
These are things anyone with the right money can enjoy,
but money doesn't make you special, it just makes you rich.
 What Hollywood shows you is an illusion,
 a sad, plastic dream.
So do what you can with your outside if you must,
but don't lose any sleep over it,
and don't spend years beating yourself up in the mirror.
Work on your inner beauty instead,
that quality we all possess.
You have to find it
 sometimes deep,
 sometimes near,
 but trust me, it's there.

THE FINISH LINE

Someday, I hope to live without fear,
without anger
and a million regrets.
I have tried to achieve this over decades
seeking wisdom through self-help,
through no help,
through higher powers and lower devils,
through short-cuts and detours,
each much harder than I thought.
Despite this, I've made progress:
    I can see it in your eyes,
    can read it in your mind.
Yet these things I hope to live without still intrude,
stumbling me as I stagger toward the finish line.
And as the end approaches,
the thought hits me:

    I was never supposed to live without these things—
    I was supposed to live *through* them.

THE SECRET TO HAPPINESS

The secret to happiness is
do what you love.
    Everything else
    only gets in the way.

THE WIZARD SAID

Long have I been a seeker of wisdom,
of hidden paths and ways.
So it was in my travels I grew weary of a world
that did not understand me—nor I, it.
In time I sought out the Wizard,
a fellow spirit cloaked in flesh,
a man wanting little and rejecting much.
He invited me to his hut,
the one on the pale mountain under the moonlit sky.
We sat by the fire sharing wine, sharing silence.
Soon, I felt brave enough to talk.
> "There are too few like us," I said.
> "Tell me why that is."
The Wizard stoked the fire,
crackling wood and curling smoke.
When he spoke, his voice was weary but not broken:
> "Weep for this world!
> Weep for those who are, yet cannot be.
> Weep for the young, the old,
> and most of all, the in-between!
> Those who should know better,
> who should seize the time they have left . . .
> The young are not wise enough,
> the old not strong enough
> to change,
> to be."

"This is true," I said. "But surely we can help them?"
The Wizard shook his head.

> "No, my friend.
> We can only help ourselves—
> and through that,
> inspire others.
> Anything else is madness!
> That you have found your path is enough.
> Let the others find theirs, or be lost."

I stared into the fire a long time,
and thought of you.

MESSAGE IN A BOTTLE

Walking on the beach
we've all thought
how great it would be to find
a message in a bottle:
    a message of secret knowledge,
    of treasure waiting to be found.
We can spend our whole lives waiting
or we can realize
our mind is the bottle.

FOREVER YOUNG

I don't want to "grow up,"
but I don't mind growing old
as long as my inner child remains
   untouched,
   unscathed,
   unbent,
   unbroken by this life
     by everyone
     and everything in it.
I want to know joy and wonder,
experiencing them all my days,
and I want you to experience them too
as we grow old but stay
forever young.

ADVICE FOR THE WITHERED SOUL

Experience teaches the only way
to get past a problem you cannot go around
is to go through it:
    headlong,
        headstrong,
powering your way to the result you want.
This is how the great become greater
and the weak become strong.
This is how we learn.
This is how we grow
    like flowers toward
        the Light.

SELF-WORTH

Too many people seek self-worth
from external sources,
but these are outside our control.
True self-worth comes
when we love, respect,
and forgive ourselves.

HARD TO BE BOTH

The artist struggles to be a man
while the man struggles to be an artist.
It is hard to be both at the same time,
to have one foot in this world
and the other in your imagination.
Few artists deal well with the world
and few men tap the full potential of their imagination.
The best of us find some kind of balance,
but there is no clear path,
no easy answers.

Welcome to the struggle.

WEATHERING THE STORM

In the storm of your heart sails a perfect soul,
  Buffeted, besieged
    but ultimately unsinkable.

DON'T LISTEN TO THEM

By whose standards will you judge yourself:
    Theirs or yours?
Don't give up, don't give in,
Just keep on getting better
everyday.

NEVER TOO LATE

Think about your life
and the people in it:
    The choices you make,
    the choices you don't
    because there's still time to change.
You are not a lost cause.
No more than I,
no more than any of us.

You're Better than You Think

The power to be awesome is hidden inside us all.
It's something we're born with,
but we have to find it.
We have to look hard,
some more than others,
me more than most.
But it's there,
and when we find it,
when we finally know how *awesome* we are,
   a thousand suns shine,
   a million rays warm us with a heat that matches our own.
Take that fire, use it!
Burn away impossibility,
   burn away everything
   that isn't awesome,
   that isn't you.

Do Something

Do something:
It doesn't have to be the right thing,
the perfect thing.
It just has to be some *thing*.
Something you mean to be good,
to matter to yourself,
to others.
Doing that one thing
transcends thoughts,
transcends words.
It moves you forward
into the Light.

CLIMB!

Those who dream:
    those who dare are watching,
    waiting for you to join them
    high above it all.
The climb is hard,
but it begins for you the same way
it began for them:
    by seizing the first rung of the ladder,
    by never giving up,
    and never letting go.
Is your grip secure?
Have you packed your courage?
Good.

    Now climb!

NOW OR NEVER

I am about to leap off a cliff.
I know I will fall,
but how long before I fly up
to claim my reward?
This is the question we all must face—
    either to be a success, or simply dead.
The businessman knows it,
    the artist,
    the author,
    the actor,
all those who dare to do more than dream.
Now look at your life and ask yourself:
    "Do I know it?"
Come, the cliff is waiting . . .
I will meet you there.

THE MUSE

The Muse strikes hard and fast,
    without fail,
    without compromise,
    firing words into my brain
    like bullets.
This is when ideas flow free
    and poems come easy.
This is that genius moment
    too seldom grasped,
    too often chased.
You cannot catch the Muse.
The Muse catches you.

IDEAS ARE MY CHILDREN

My brain is pregnant
with a million ideas:
   stories
      poems
         dreams.
It would take a thousand lifetimes
to give birth to them all,
so I must choose carefully
which children I bring into this world.
Sometimes they are the best,
sometimes merely the easiest,
but they are all reflections of me.

INSPIRED

To be inspired is to be lifted up,
transported to realms
where anything is possible.
These places exist
where they have always existed:
    inside you,
        outside you,
            and beyond.
Realms of pure imagination
where you can create at your highest level
with your Higher Self.
Seize your vision, shape it,
now bring it back to our world,
guiding it from a single idea
into an empire.

THE CREATIVE SPIRIT

Great ideas never die,
   They simply wait to be born—
      if not to one parent, then the next.

THE FIRST DAY

They say, "Today is the first day of the rest of your life."
So why aren't you running around
    fucking
    drinking
    finding yourself in the company of others?
Maybe it's because you want to be alone
to feel something only I can give you,
the kind of release that's less showy, more secret.
    The slow burn,
    that "a-ha!" moment where something shakes loose
    and you feel your true self, your true power.
That's the real you, carefree and beautiful:
    the brilliant you,
    the God-You,
    the Soul-You,
    the innocent spirit that yearns to express itself.
So put down this poem and
    BE THAT YOU,
the one you were meant to be
from the moment
you first came into this life.

Be the Magic

To be alive must mean something more
    than to not be dead.
It must mean believing in yourself
    and what you do.
To be truly alive,
    you must not just feel the magic,
    you must *be* the magic,
    creating wonder for others
    even as you experience it for yourself.
That is a life well-lived,
    a destiny fulfilled.
Though sometimes the magic dims,
    it is never gone for good.
Remember that—
    draw strength from it,
    and know that your magic is still there,
    waiting to be used.

THAT GENIUS MOMENT

There is a profound satisfaction
    when everything comes together like magic,
        as if there could be
            no other time,
                no other way
                    than now.

THE ONLY COMPETITION

They say it's hard to make it as a writer,
    much less a poet.
There's "too much competition"
    and it's hard to stand out.
Well, that's true for quitters,
    for people with only one book in them
    or no patience to work toward their dream.
The truth is, if you're good,
    if you're persistent and prolific,
    if you know the social media game,
    eventually, your work will stand out
    and you'll realize
    the only competition
    you have left is yourself.

THIS MAN I'VE BECOME

I am so proud of myself, this man I've become:
    this poet, this writer,
    this Weaver of Dreams.
I have shaped this destiny from nothing,
    from mere wisps of hope—
    fantasies in the moonlight.
I've worked my magic,
made it real now,
    blazing in the sun
    as I take my place
    next to my idols,
    an icon at last.

HOW TO BE A CELEBRITY

What looks effortless now
  took decades to perfect.
    I used my pain
      to become something more,
        not something less.

GODLIKE

I could have been so many things.
Instead, I am this:
    a sculptor of thoughts,
        shaper of words.
I see the invisible, the impossible,
visions of What Never Was and Will Always Be!
Magic, conjured things:
    dreams,
        desires.
These are the clay my hands work,
the miracle my mind breathes
as I sit Godlike
in my room.

MY WORDS, MY GIFT

When I write poems,
I am not myself anymore.
I am you, reading them.
I am the world, loving them.
Until finally, I am my spirit, leaving them.
My words remain where I cannot,
my gift to you.

   Enjoy.

ABOUT THE AUTHOR

Jackson Dean Chase brings you Bold Visions of Dark Places. He is the author of *Bukowski's Ghost: Poems for Old Souls in New Bodies*, *Love at the Bottom of the Litter Box: Bukowski, Cats, and Me*, and *Christmas Eve in the Drunk Tank (and Other Horrible Holiday Poems)*. When not creating poetry, Jackson writes Young Adult fiction and non-fiction self-help books for writers.

Thank you for buying *Be the Magic!*

If you enjoyed this book, please leave an online review. Even if it's just a few lines, your words can make a difference reaching new readers.

Have a question or suggestion? Or just want to say hi?

Jackson loves to connect with his fans! Friend or follow him online.

Website: JacksonDeanChase.com

Facebook: facebook.com/jacksondeanchase

Tumblr: JacksonDeanChase.tumblr.com

Twitter: @Jackson_D_Chase

Email: jackson@jacksondeanchase.com

Want to know when Jackson's next book is coming out?

Sign up and get **FREE BOOKS** at: **www.JacksonDeanChase.com**

There's NO SPAM, and your email address will never be shared.

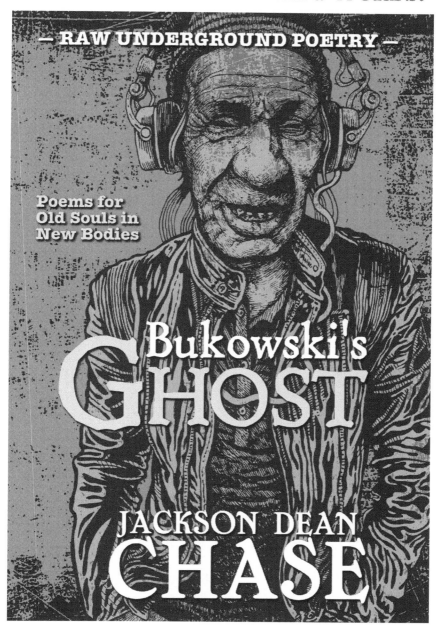

People love me. People hate me. And I do a little of both. What you are about to read is my personal poetry. Words I bled for, words I own as much as they own me. With them, you can see not just into the deepest part of my soul, but into your own darkness, your own light. You might be surprised what you find . . .

— **Jackson Dean Chase**

ANOTHER WASTED NIGHT

I am drunk on regret, on knowing
I'll never be good enough.
This diner is old, comforting,
like my mother's hands.
I slide into a booth and order fries
wanting to taste love,
wanting to taste anything
but what I feel right now.

TRUE POEMS

True poems are not safe:
    They must murder some part of you
        while giving birth to another . . .

Love at the Bottom of the Litter Box collects every poem by Jackson Dean Chase that mentions cats, including these soulful gems:

You Had Me at "Meow"

You had me at "meow," my friend.
You had me with three sleepy blinks,
with the tender flick of your tail,
the purr in your throat.
You had me with all these things:
treasured moments
curling in my lap.

Today

Today is the day when love lies dreaming
 as Mexicans cut my grass,
 as cats yowl and dogs bark,
 as the phone rings and bills mount,
 as my parents inch toward their graves,
 and I speed toward mine,
 somewhere, a girl thinks of me
 and I, of her.
We shared something once,
a moment of passion.
Now we share this memory
and wonder what might have been . . .

WHO STUFFED YOUR STOCKING?

— RAW UNDERGROUND POETRY —

CHRISTMAS EVE in the
DRUNK TANK
and Other Horrible Holiday Poems

JACKSON DEAN
CHASE

Best Selling Author of BUKOWSKI'S GHOST

For some, the holidays are a time of hope. For others, a time of dark-
ness . . . This winter-themed chapbook is soaked in beer and madness!

CHRISTMAS EVE
IN THE DRUNK TANK *

Eight tiny reindeer pull
the sleigh of my soul,
caroling madly from this bar to that.
   It's a party,
     an endless party!
   So pick your poison,
     pour your pleasure!
We're celebrating our survival,
but not everyone is happy
to see that we've made it:
   the boss says don't leave early,
   the wife says don't be late,
   and the law—the motherfucking law—
   says don't feel too free,
   or WE'LL GETCHA!
     We'll punch out your lights and
     stick you in a cracked gray room
     that smells like piss,
     where the only bars are on the doors,
     and the only buddies you got
     are a buncha jerks
     who hate yer guts . . .

(* poem continues in the book)

Made in the USA
Middletown, DE
15 April 2017